# B
# READING

• FROM BRF •

FOR SUMMER

Text copyright © BRF 2002

**Published by**
**The Bible Reading Fellowship**
First Floor, Elsfield Hall
15–17 Elsfield Way, Oxford OX2 8FG
ISBN 1 84101 310 2

First published 2002
10 9 8 7 6 5 4 3 2 1 0
All rights reserved

A catalogue record for this book is available from the British Library

Printed and bound in Great Britain by
Bookmarque, Croydon

# CONTENTS

# GENERAL INTRODUCTION

 Welcome to the Summer edition of BRF's Bible reading sampler. We think you'll find something to enjoy here, whether it's a taste of our regular Bible reading notes, an extract from one of our *People's Bible Commentary volumes*, or simply finding out more about the range of publications that we produce.

At BRF we are passionate about helping people grow in personal Bible reading and prayer, as well as in being a member of the Christian Church. By reading the Bible, we grow in the knowledge of how our faith fits together, and this nurtures our prayer life, both as individuals and as worshipping communities. And reading with the help of insightful comment from others can help us get deeper into God's word, challenge our assumptions and bring us fresh insights into familiar passages.

*Naomi Starkey*

Naomi Starkey
Managing Editor, Bible reading notes

# New Daylight

*New Daylight* is ideal for those looking for a devotional approach to reading and understanding the Bible. Each issue covers four months of daily Bible readings and reflection from a regular team of contributors, who have represented a stimulating mix of church backgrounds, from Baptist to Anglican Franciscan. Each day's reading provides a Bible passage (text included), helpful comment and prayer or thought for reflection. In *New Daylight* the Sundays and special festivals from the Church calendar are noted on the relevant days, offering a chance to get acquainted with the rich traditions of the Christian year. Our *New Daylight* extract is from the May–August 2002 notes, on the theme 'John the Baptist'. The comment is written by Adrian Plass, an internationally popular writer and speaker, and author of *When You Walk* (BRF, 1997) and *The Unlocking* (reissued in 2002).

# He was the answer to a prayer

Then an angel of the Lord appeared... When Zechariah saw him, he was... gripped with fear. But the angel said... 'Do not be afraid... your prayer has been heard. Your wife Elizabeth will bear you a son, and you are to give him the name John.' ... Zechariah asked the angel, 'How can I be sure of this? I am an old man and my wife is well on in years.' The angel answered, 'I am Gabriel. I stand in the presence of God, and I have been sent... to tell you this good news. And now you will be silent and not able to speak until the day this happens, because you did not believe my words.'

If you get the time, read the whole of this story, verses 5–20.

Can you blame Gabriel for taking such action? Angels do have a rough time occasionally. Imagine turning up full of enthusiasm to tell one of these awkward humans that, against the odds, he's going to have a son. Also, that this son will be great in the sight of God and filled with the Holy Spirit from birth and he'll bring lots of Israelites back to the Lord. Oh, and he'll be the one who prepares the way for the Messiah. All these good things and you get such a wet reaction from the said human.

You might think Zechariah would be just a bit pleased. Instead, the nervous old priest mumbles about feeling unsure about this because he and his wife are well on in years and so it's unlikely... No wonder Gabriel draws himself to his full height and lays down the law in no uncertain fashion. Perhaps he felt he'd been too soft all those years ago when Gideon came out with the same sort of rubbish. Is it possible that angels learn?

The really interesting aspect of the whole business is that, as Gabriel makes quite clear, Elizabeth's pregnancy and the birth of John would be a direct answer to Zechariah's own prayer. It is probably the thing that he and his wife wanted most in the world. Now that he is being offered his heart's desire, he doubts God has sufficient power to make it happen.

It's a lesson to all of us. Prayer is dangerous. We may talk to God about a particular need for years and simply get into the habit of believing it will never be answered. Not a good idea. Remember Zechariah!

### Reflection

*Be careful with prayers—they might be answered.*

# He was loved and wanted

'He will be a joy and delight to you, and many will rejoice because of his birth.' After this his wife Elizabeth became pregnant and for five months remained in seclusion. 'The Lord has done this for me,' she said. 'In these days he has shown his favour and taken away my disgrace among the people.'

I was discussing with a friend recently whether or not he and I would have chosen to have children if we had seen our future with them in advance. We agreed that, probably, neither of us would have proceeded if we had. It's not, you understand, that our children have not been a joy and delight to us. They have been in their own particular ways, sometimes wonderfully so, but they've been other things as well. So many emotional cliffhangers, so many alarms and excursions, so much worry of various kinds. Of course you forget all that when things are good, but, yes, a clear and detailed vision of the future might have put me off altogether.

God was very good to this elderly couple. Once Zechariah had got over his negative response to the good news, he must have remembered and relished that promise from God that John was going to be a joy and delight to his parents. How wonderful for that fact to be furnished in advance from the most reputable source of all. As for Elizabeth, she was like a football manager whose team has just beaten Manchester United—over the moon. After years of barrenness, a son! A gift from God in the autumn of her life.

God gave John the best possible start for the tough times that were to come, didn't he? It is hard to imagine a son ever having been wanted more than this one. Being loved and wanted was the best possible launching pad for the rest of John's life. Indeed, being valued and appreciated is rocket fuel for the future of any child.

We must be very tender with those who have not had this kind of start. It's all very well to say how fellow believers should behave, but if you've never been loved it really is ever so hard to be good.

### Prayer

*Father, may those whose hearts were broken before they even started learn what it means to be loved by you.*

# He was filled with the Holy Spirit

When Elizabeth heard Mary's greeting, the baby leaped in her womb, and Elizabeth was filled with the Holy Spirit. In a loud voice she exclaimed: 'Blessed are you among women, and blessed is the child you will bear! But why am I so favoured, that the mother of my Lord should come to me? As soon as the sound of your greeting reached my ears, the baby in my womb leaped for joy. Blessed is she who has believed that what the Lord has said to her will be accomplished!'

Gabriel had promised that John would be filled with the Holy Spirit from birth, but it seems to have started even before that. In this, one of my favourite gospel moments, we learn that as the two pregnant women met, the unborn John seemed to recognize the unborn Jesus. The foetus inside Elizabeth jumped with a sudden spiritual awareness that the reason for his very existence was only inches away, in that younger, equally excited mother-to-be. I don't know if the presence of the Holy Spirit has an infectious quality, but it appears like that here, doesn't it? Suddenly Elizabeth is speaking inspired words, closely followed by Mary's famous hymn of praise. What a party! Both pregnant, both filled with the Spirit, both filled with babies filled with the Spirit, one bearing God himself within her body.

Much modern teaching about the Holy Spirit has attempted to set down processes or specific stages in connection with the moment when the Spirit enters a believer's life. Such teaching tends to draw heavily on events in the book of Acts and on sections of Paul's letters. Well, that's all right, as long as we don't end up tidying God and his way with us out of existence. I am afraid, brothers and sisters, that God does what he likes. You may have noticed that. It would be very helpful to the Church as a whole if we abandoned the notion that theology can be kept in a paddock at the back of the house, and taken out for a bit of a gallop twice a week.

Anything can happen if we are open to being filled with the Spirit at any time.

### Prayer

*We long to be filled with the Spirit and to speak out your words, Lord.*

# He was his own man

In those days John the Baptist came, preaching in the Desert of Judea and saying, 'Repent, for the kingdom of heaven is near.' … John's clothes were made of camel's hair, and he had a leather belt round his waist. His food was locusts and wild honey. People went out to him from Jerusalem and all Judea and the whole region of the Jordan. Confessing their sins, they were baptized by him in the Jordan river.

What do Christians look like? How do they do their hair? How do they speak? How do they walk and eat and drink and sing and play Monopoly? Is there a distinctive Christian style to fit all these activities? There certainly has been, in this country at any rate, but it is less and less the case nowadays. Huddling together in conformity of dress and generally narrow lifestyles is not productive in terms of what the gospel demands. I am glad that religious cloning is gradually becoming a thing of the past. Of course, we are unified (one hopes) by a love for Jesus, each other and a desire to follow Jesus obediently, but those features can be expressed in a diversity of personal styles and approaches.

Having said this, a friend of mine is clearly not thrilled with this new acceptance. Having battled pleasurably through the 1960s and 1970s against elders who objected to his exceptionally long hair, he now finds himself not only accepted but invited to join the leadership team! Will he be able to overcome his disappointment?

As well as being God's man, John was his own man. Well-educated and competent, he chose to adopt an environment, diet and way of dressing that, although bizarre, related specifically to the task in hand and he wasn't interested in what others thought about it. We have to be careful, don't we? We may not like the way a person dresses, how he expresses himself, the details of his lifestyle or some of the places he frequents, but we are to estimate others (if at all) only on the basis of their love for God and their obedience to his call. How would John the Baptist get on at your next 'bring and share' lunch?

### Prayer
*Lord, may we welcome the richness of variety in your family.*

# He was aggressive and uncompromising

But when he saw many of the Pharisees and Sadducees coming to where he was baptizing, he said to them: 'You brood of vipers! Who warned you to flee from the coming wrath? Produce fruit in keeping with repentance. And do not think that you can say to yourselves, "We have Abraham as our father." I tell you that out of these stones God can raise up children for Abraham. The axe is already at the root of the trees, and every tree that does not produce good fruit will be cut down and thrown into the fire.'

John really laid into the Pharisees and Sadducees. Not only did he call them names, but he predicted what they'd probably claim about their spiritual heritage and why what they said would be wrong. His comment about the stones must have infuriated them. How I wish I'd been there. I wouldn't have been a Pharisee or a Sadducee, of course—I would have been a humble ordinary person, just as I'm sure you would.

One of my abiding fears is that, as a Church, we let God down by refusing to take this kind of aggressive stance when the time is right. We are handicapped by the disease of politeness. We get cross about the machinations of those newly arrived upstarts on the flower rota or the movement of some dreary picture to a spot ten feet from where it has hung for the last 30 years. Meanwhile there are political, social and spiritual issues crying out for comment from those of us who claim or want to represent God's viewpoint.

Being a Christian is not about being nice to people, nor, obviously, is it about being nasty. It is about seeing what the Father is doing and then joining in. That's what John did imperfectly and Jesus perfectly. It is quite frightening and quite exciting.

Let's all pray that we will be more open to the prompting of the Holy Spirit. Beware, though. When that prayer is answered, some of us will have to turn away from that flower rota and instead get tough with the people and institutions that really need it.

**Prayer**
*Help us to be ready to speak out at the right time.*

# He was a practical and specific moralist

'What shall we do then?' the crowd asked. John answered, 'The man with two tunics should share with him who has none, and the one who has food should do the same.' Tax collectors also came to be baptized. 'Teacher,' they asked, 'what should we do?' 'Don't collect any more than you are required to,' he told them. Then some soldiers asked him, 'And what should we do?' He replied, 'Don't extort money and don't accuse people falsely—be content with your pay.'

Well, they did ask! It strikes me that John, like Jesus, might be less popular in our modern Western churches than one might suppose. Imagine if John the Baptist came along to the local church one Sunday morning and was asked similar questions by a bunch of people thinking about being baptized. 'What should we do?' they would ask.

'Right!' John would say briskly, 'if you've got two cars, give one to a family that can't afford one or, if you like, sell one of them and give the money to an aid agency or something. Some of you have got far too much money stashed away as well. God gave it to you to use for others. Are you going to?'

'What should I do?' another person would ask.

'Stop being selfish and ratty with your wife when no one else is around and show a bit of affection,' John would suggest.

'What about me?'

'Dump your pornography.'

'And me?'

'Keep your promise about visiting the elderly lady next door every day. You've stopped going.'

Terrifying, isn't it, just thinking about what might happen? (And if you think I'm going to say where I come in that list, think again!)

Of course, I made all that up. I haven't the faintest idea what John or Jesus would say if they turned up in the flesh at my church or any other church. We are low on practical morality, though, don't you think? In our modern, pussyfooting set-ups we Christians can get away with murder or, at least, we can bury the body without being seen by anyone else—except Jesus. Think on.

## A confession

*Lord, we call you Lord,*
*but you are not Lord in our lives.*

# He accepted truth, however strange

Then John gave this testimony: 'I saw the Spirit come down from heaven as a dove and remain on him. I would not have known him, except that the one who sent me to baptize with water told me, "The man on whom you see the Spirit come down and remain is he who will baptize with the Holy Spirit." I have seen and I testify that this is the Son of God.'

Now, let's just think this through. Mary and Elizabeth were related, and we know that, in a sense, John and Jesus met before either of them was born. Surely it is inconceivable that the cousins failed to meet when they were growing up in separate but not inaccessibly distant parts of the country. They must have known each other. The manner and depth of their relationship is not something we can discover, but, from John's words, it seems that he was not fully or perhaps even partially aware that Jesus was the Messiah. Given the nature of both men, this seems strange. Nevertheless, it appears to be the case.

How remarkable, then, that, on seeing the Spirit alight on Jesus in the form of a dove, John immediately accepted that this familiar figure, this cousin of his, this son of Mary and Joseph, was the Son of God, the one whose way it had been his task to prepare. I wonder, might there have been just a single instant of jaw-dropping amazement as he registered the fact that God become man had been so close to him for so long? 'Oh! It's you…!'

An ongoing problem in the Church is the reluctance of many of us to allow that God may significantly use individuals who are of little worth in our eyes. I warn you and I warn myself that there is no class system in the kingdom of God. The person who sits three seats away from me every Sunday, the person whom I regard with indulgence or pity or slight scorn or I barely notice because his or her face is so very familiar, may be the very person God selects to speak his will or his discipline or his comfort to me. He who has ears…

### Prayer

*Forgive our religious snobbery, Lord. Open our ears and eyes.*

# He was strong enough to be flexible

Then Jesus came from Galilee to the Jordan to be baptized by John. But John tried to deter him, saying, 'I need to be baptized by you, and do you come to me?' Jesus replied, 'Let it be so now; it is proper for us to do this to fulfil all righteousness.' Then John consented.

A mighty hush must have descended over the hosts of heaven as this extraordinary rehearsal of death and resurrection was carried out. There can have been few more dramatic moments in the history of the world, and this one would not have been possible if John had not been ready and willing to be corrected in his assumption that it should have been the other way round. Fierce, focused and fanatical as he may have appeared to some, John was actually a man under authority who knew that orders from the highest source, however surprising, must be obeyed. It is so terribly easy for any of us to lock ourselves into an agenda or a process that was begun by God and refuse to come out even when the Holy Spirit himself issues orders for change.

When I began to write, I had a great deal to say about the emphasis placed by certain sections of the Church on the avoidance of drinking, smoking and other such fundamentally neutral activities. The gospel is primarily about letting off spectacular fireworks; it is not about stamping on sparklers. I believe it was quite right for me to say these things, and I shall go on saying them as long as there are those who use the beating out of sin as an excuse for avoiding the awesome tasks that God has ready for them.

However, some time ago, an elderly lady wrote me a charmingly supportive letter, concluding with a plea that I should not joke quite so much about alcohol. Her son was an alcoholic and had made several suicide attempts. I receive a number of letters telling me what I should do or think or say. I ignore most of them, but this was a rebuke couched in love and God spoke to me through it. May he also grant me the strength and humility to be like John and to do what I'm told.

### Reflection

*Lord, too often it is my agenda I pay attention to, not yours.*

# He wasn't possessive of men or ministry

The next day John was there again with two of his disciples. When he saw Jesus passing by, he said, 'Look, the Lamb of God!' When the two disciples heard him say this, they followed Jesus. Turning round, Jesus saw them following and asked, 'What do you want?' They said 'Rabbi' (which means Teacher), 'where are you staying?' 'Come,' he replied, 'and you will see.' So they went and saw where he was staying, and spent that day with him.

I know of a Christian leader who told his followers that if they transferred their allegiance to someone else, they would lose the blessing of God. Perhaps he should read this passage from John's Gospel. Hold on, what am I talking about? He probably uses it to support his position.

Superficially it appears a sad little story. John points out to his disciples that the man passing is the Son of God and, suddenly, they've gone! From that day onwards they seem to have become disciples of Jesus instead of John. They had been with the one who was preparing the way. Now they have gone to be with The Way.

Well, it would be a sad story if we thought that John was upset by their decision. I don't believe he was. I believe that, for John, this episode would have been a microcosm of the process that was inevitable, given the nature of his calling. Losing two disci-ples to Jesus was not a tragedy. It was a triumph for the plan that God had set in motion before John was born, and if John had had an ounce of pride in his locust and honey-nourished body, he might have considered it a personal triumph—the visible fulfilment of his ministry.

If it had been a contemporary fashion, I reckon John might have thrust his fist in the air at that point and cried 'Yes!!'

It's very hard to hand on the baton sometimes, but if our leg of the relay is run, we must rejoice in the eventual outcome of the race or face the fact that we never really wanted to belong to a team. Let's give up grace-fully when our time comes.

### Prayer

*For what we have been allowed to do, may the Lord make us truly thankful.*

# He was human and vulnerable

When John heard in prison what Christ was doing, he sent his disciples to ask him, 'Are you the one who was to come, or should we expect someone else?' Jesus replied, 'Go back and report to John what you hear and see: the blind receive sight, the lame walk, those who have leprosy are cured, the deaf hear, the dead are raised, and the good news is preached to the poor.'

The devil tells lies in the darkness, doesn't he?

Sometimes, after a particularly successful evening in which I have made an impassioned plea for those present to respond to the love of God, I lie in the darkness of some obscure hotel room and ask myself if I have been talking complete nonsense.

How could John the Baptist possibly have plummeted to such a depth of doubt? After all, it hadn't been long since he had been proclaiming the need for repentance, aggressively taking on the Pharisees and Sadducees and baptizing hundreds in the waters of the Jordan. Not only that, but the Holy Spirit had enabled him to identify Jesus as the Messiah on the bank of that same river. He knew that Jesus was the one who was to come. Why on earth would he for one moment believe that he should expect someone else?

The sad and salutary truth is that John was human and, as such, he was subject to all the fear and uneasiness that any human being would suffer when shut away from their place and function and the light of the outside world.

The reply that Jesus sends is sometimes quoted as an example of the contradictions to be found in the Bible. Why, the cynics want to know, does Jesus give a different answer to John than he gave to the Pharisees when they asked him the same question? Well, it is just one example of the glorious, life-giving contradictions that offer evidence of the creative, ingenious God we try to serve. Jesus didn't want to comfort the Pharisees, but he did want to comfort John. Very soon he was to have similar experiences himself.

Call out to Jesus in the darkness and listen for his message of comfort.

**Prayer**

*Lord, I'll try to do my best. Catch me when I fall.*

# He inspired passion (1)

Jesus began to speak to the crowd about John: 'What did you go out into the desert to see? A reed swayed by the wind? If not, what did you go out to see? A man dressed in fine clothes? No, those who wear fine clothes are in kings' palaces... A prophet? Yes, I tell you, and more than a prophet. This is the one about whom it is written: "I will send my messenger ahead of you, who will prepare your way before you." I tell you the truth: among those born of women there has not risen anyone greater than John the Baptist; yet he who is least in the kingdom of heaven is greater than he.'

This speech, delivered by Jesus as John's disciples hurried back towards Herod's prison with the Lord's answer to their master's question, has haunted me ever since I first read it more than 30 years ago. As with so many of the gospel stories, and not least because of the literary style of the day, some of the most important truths seem to dwell between the lines.

Why do I sense unshed tears in the eyes of Jesus as he begins this impassioned speech about the man who was his cousin, his forerunner and his friend? Why can I almost hear the catch in his voice as he quotes the scripture that prophesies the coming of John? Do I sense his sadness at the thought of John, once so confident in his proclamations, now worried about whether or not Jesus really is the one for whom all his work was a preparation? Was he aware that this wild light would soon be extinguished? Was Jesus grieving for those who, over the centuries, would suffer pain and darkness and early death in order that the gospel should be preached?

I pray that you and I might inspire passion in the heart of our Saviour. Not by getting everything right, because we won't; not by understanding all that happens to us, because that will not be possible, but by doing the job we have been given as well as it can be done in the light of what we know and by calling out to him for the warm glow of his reassurance when darkness falls.

### Prayer

*Give us the same passion for you as you have for us.*

# He was disciplined in his role

'To what can I compare this generation? They are like children sitting in the marketplaces and calling out to others: "We played the flute for you, and you did not dance; we sang a dirge, and you did not mourn." For John came neither eating nor drinking, and they say, "He has a demon." The Son of Man came eating and drinking, and they say, "Here is a glutton and a drunkard, a friend of tax collectors and 'sinners'." But wisdom is proved right by her actions.'

I am reluctant to write on this subject, being one of the least disciplined people I know. When I say this to people they laugh and ask how can I possibly get books written without discipline? The answer is that my motivation is a compound of fear that the job will never get done, a panic-stricken desire to be obedient and the deadline date printed so irrevocably in my contract. I do it, but my discipline is a small boat in a howling storm. I hope and believe that God can live with this arrangement.

John the Baptist was not like me at all, except in the sense that he was like all followers of Jesus. I mean that each of us has a role and a task or succession of tasks assigned by God and, by any means that do not contravene the laws of love, we must live out that role and fulfil those tasks. John was highly disciplined in his personal habits, as Jesus points out in this passage, and that particular way of living was appropriate to the job that God had given him. Jesus was able to eat and drink, go to parties and visit friends and have expensive ointment poured over his hair and feet because his fundamental task was to be himself—a free human being, fettered only to the continually revealed will of his father.

Take heart! You and I may sometimes feel we are only managing to do the job by the skin of our spiritual teeth, but, as always, God looks into our hearts and is pleased with an intention to do what we are told. He has learned to live with the scrambled means by which we attempt to be obedient.

### Prayer
*Lord, help me to do my bit.*

# He inspired passion (2)

On Herod's birthday the daughter of Herodias danced for them and pleased Herod so much that he promised with an oath to give her whatever she asked. Prompted by her mother, she said, 'Give me here on a platter the head of John the Baptist.' The king was distressed, but because of his oaths and his dinner guests, he ordered that her request be granted and had John beheaded in the prison. His head was brought in on a platter and given to the girl, who carried it to her mother.

John inspired passion in the heart of Herodias, but it was nothing to do with love. Rather, it was a wild hatred, the result of John's outspoken remarks about the unsuitability of her marriage to Herod. This passage tells us that Herod also wanted John dead, but was afraid to do the deed because popular opinion held him to be a prophet.

When hatred and weakness knot themselves together like a pair of snakes, disaster occurs before long. In our own age Nazi Germany is a grim reminder of what can happen. Here, because Herod was showing off in front of his guests and making extravagant promises to the daughter of Herodias, he destroyed John and also any chance of benefiting from contact with him. It may be pure conjecture, but perhaps Herod regretted the outcome of his thoughtless behaviour for reasons other than fear of the people. Perhaps he had developed a respect for John and was hoping that his prisoner would have something important to say to him. If so, he had blown it.

I don't have many opportunities for beheading people as a favour to others, nor do those I dislike tend to come to such a grisly end, but I cannot escape awareness in my own life of the way in which this deadly cocktail of weakness and passion can work. I have learned to be wary of opportunities to indulge any kind of inappropriate passion. It would be so easy—like poor old Esau with his soup—to give up the most important things in the world in exchange for a passing fancy. If that is what you are considering doing at the moment, please think again.

### Prayer

*Protect us against our own weaknesses. Help us to be strong.*

# He was mourned

John's disciples came and took his body and buried it. Then they went and told Jesus. When Jesus heard what had happened, he withdrew by boat privately to a solitary place. Hearing of this, the crowds followed him on foot from the towns. When Jesus landed and saw a large crowd, he had compassion on them and healed their sick.

A few simple words don't convey very much, but we can guess and imagine. John's disciples took their master's body and buried it. Did they weep as they performed that sad task? Did they stand around the tomb or grave afterwards and ask themselves and each other what it had all been about? Who had this strange, dynamic, driven leader of theirs really been? Had he been right in the things he preached and said? Where was he now? What of the future? What should they do and where should they go? There was no one to give them the answers to those questions now that John had gone. First of all, they had to tell Jesus.

I wonder if he already knew? The idea that Jesus was aware of everything without having to be told is clearly not supported by scripture. He is said, for instance, to have been 'astonished' on a couple of occasions, and, of course, he could not be truly man as well as God if he was unable to experience or understand the shock of sudden realization or knowledge. It seems that special insights were doled out to him, as it were, when they became necessary.

Besides, one brief glimpse of John's wretchedly unhappy disciples as they approached must have given him a very big clue as to what they were about to say. Was there more weeping? Did Jesus place comforting hands on the arms and bowed shoulders of these men who had lost their master? I think so.

Then Jesus, deeply moved by his cousin's death, looked for just a few moments alone with his grief. Sitting in a little boat in a quiet place with his head in his hands, he mourned his loss.

He was not alone for long. The crowds found him. The crowds always found him. He must have let out a deep sigh, then business as usual.

### Prayer

*Thank you for being as human as you are divine.*

# Guidelines

*Guidelines* is a unique Bible reading resource that offers four months of in-depth study written by leading scholars. Contributors are drawn from around the world as well as the UK, and represent a stimulating and thought-provoking breadth of Christian tradition. Instead of dated daily readings, *Guidelines* provides weekly units, broken into at least six sections, plus an introduction giving context for the passage, and a final section of points for thought and prayer. On any day you can read as many or as few sections as you wish. As well as a copy of *Guidelines*, you will need a Bible, as the passage is not included. The *Guidelines* extract in this sampler, on the theme 'The Holy Spirit in Luke', is by Michael Harper, who is the Dean of the British Antiochian Orthodox Deanery.

# The Holy Spirit in Luke's Gospel

Most are agreed that Luke was the author of this Gospel, and is the person Paul calls 'the good physician' (Colossians 4:14). Each book of the New Testament was written with a purpose in mind, and it is particularly true of this one. It has several unique features, but one stands out. Luke wrote a sequel, the Acts of the Apostles. He makes it clear that the Ascension of Christ was not the end of the story—far from it. Nor indeed was Acts 28 the last chapter in the story of the Church. Christ's presence and power continues in the Church, and it all flows on, right to the twenty-first century and beyond. Luke is concerned to show how the gospel of Christ spread from Jerusalem to Rome in one generation.

Just as the Acts of the Apostles has been called 'the Acts of the Holy Spirit', so Luke's Gospel focuses often on the Holy Spirit's presence and influence. Also we can see that Luke has a mission agenda. First of all he shows how the way was prepared for Christ, and then how Christ prepared the way for the coming of the Holy Spirit at Pentecost. Yesterday was Pentecost Sunday in both the Western and the Eastern calendars. But in the Eastern tradition, Pentecost Sunday is the equivalent of Trinity Sunday. It is today—called the Monday of the Holy Spirit—that the Orthodox churches celebrate the Holy Spirit. Finally Luke shows how the church, inspired by the Holy Spirit, burst out of its Jewish foundations, and became transcultural.

The notes are based on the New International Version (NIV).

## 1 The Forerunner

Luke 1:5–25, 39–45

In the Orthodox Church John the Baptist is called the 'Forerunner' and holds a place of special honour. In most of their churches his icon is placed next to Jesus Christ's. The passages we have read tell us about his mother Elizabeth, his father Zechariah, and his conception. We notice immediately the important role of the Holy Spirit in the life of John the Baptist. The angel tells Zechariah that 'he will be filled with the Holy Spirit even from birth'. Later when Mary, the mother of Jesus, visits their home shortly after her own conception, we are told that the baby John 'leaped in her womb, and Elizabeth was filled with the Holy Spirit'.

Thus we see Luke's 'signature tune'—his recurring allusions to the action of the Holy Spirit—at the very beginning of the Gospel, even before Christ was born. The angel tells John's father Zechariah that his wife is to have a baby, and he is to call the child 'John'. Jesus was later to say that his cousin John was the 'greatest' of the Old Testament saints. He was greater than Moses, or Elijah. But Christ went on to say he is the least in the new covenant, since he died before the covenant was given through the Death and Resurrection of the Son of God. In the Eastern tradition great honour is given to people like Moses and Elijah. Many Orthodox Arab Christians name their sons 'Elijah'. But John the Baptist surpasses them all, and Luke makes it clear to us that it was the Holy Spirit who inspired him.

This is a special time of preparation, and John the Baptist had a key role to play as the one who would prepare the way for the coming of Christ. We can see in this story the important ministry of old people, and we shall see the same later with Simeon and the prophetess Anna. Both Elizabeth and Zechariah were 'well along in years' (v. 7). However old we may be God has his purposes for us. In an age that looks increasingly to the young, should we not also affirm the life and ministry of older people?

'The memory of the righteous is celebrated with songs of praise, but the Lord's testimony is sufficient for thee, O Forerunner' (from the Kairon, the Eastern Liturgy).


# 2 Mary's conception announced

Luke 1:26–35

The 'sixth month' refers to the pregnancy of Elizabeth. Mary was 'betrothed' or engaged to marry Joseph and, in the Jewish custom of the day, that was binding. The betrothal service was a solemn undertaking to marry, and divorce was necessary in order to break it. So we can understand the reason for the visit of an angel to Joseph, who was preparing to divorce Mary (Matthew 1:20).

We see immediately the profound modesty of Mary. She was greatly troubled when the angel Gabriel calls her 'highly favoured', and declares that 'the Lord is with you' (v. 28). On the other hand she had the confidence to make her own decision, and to make it immediately. Earlier in the Gospel Luke tells us that the angel, when he visited Zechariah, told him to call his son 'John'. So here the angel Gabriel is specific: 'You are to give him the name "Jesus"'. Still today in the Middle East naming a child carries great significance. The Orthodox attach great importance to a child's name, and only names which have Christian roots are used. If one joins the Orthodox Church from another tradition, and one does not have a traditional Christian name, then a new name is given.

In passing, it is interesting to note that in both the East and West Mary's visitation by the angel is called 'the Annunciation', and is commemorated in both traditions in the new calendar on 25 March. It is the obvious date, since it is nine months before Christmas Day—a full pregnancy term.

Mary is naturally startled by the news that she is to bear a son. Clearly the angel has convinced her that this is to happen immediately and before her marriage, otherwise her reaction would have been different. So she asks the simple question, 'How will this be, since I am a virgin?' (v. 34). The angel explains it to her as the action of the Holy Spirit, who will 'come upon you, and… will overshadow you' (v. 35).

This is not the only time that the action of the Holy Spirit is seen in terms of 'overshadowing'. As we shall see the same imagery is used at the Transfiguration of Christ. It is wonderfully reassuring to think of the Holy Spirit as over us—protecting, inspiring and changing us. Just as Christ in the words of the Nicene Creed was 'incarnate of the Holy Spirit and the Virgin Mary', so the Holy Spirit brings to birth new and exciting developments in our lives.


# 3 The Spirit of prophecy

Luke 2:25–38

In the Old Testament the prophets are linked in importance with the law. Both were inspired by the Holy Spirit. In the case of the law, there was a theophany on the holy mountain similar to the one we shall be looking at tomorrow on the banks of the Jordan.

On Sinai the symbol of the Holy Spirit was the cloud which overshadowed Moses. The New Testament makes clear that the prophets of the Old Covenant were inspired by the Holy Spirit. In 2 Peter we read 'no prophecy of Scripture came about by the prophet's own inspiration, for prophecy never had its origins in the will of man, but men spoke from God as they were carried along by the Holy Spirit' (1:20–21).

The idea, expressed by Peter, of being 'carried along' is a graphic one, and well describes this passage. We read of two elderly people being carried along by the stream of the Holy Spirit, like ships entering harbour on a spring tide. They knew exactly what they were doing, and who this young child was.

The two mentioned here are both very old. Simeon is described as 'righteous and devout'. The Holy Spirit is mentioned no fewer than three times in this short story. It is said 'the Holy Spirit was upon him', that he had had a revelation by the Holy Spirit that he would not die before he saw Christ, and that he was 'moved by the Holy Spirit' to go into the temple at that moment. We would say he was 'guided'. And from his lips came the matchless words of the Nunc Dimittis, sung regularly at Evensong or Vespers. It is often the case, too, that prophets prophesy their own deaths, and that is what Simeon did on this occasion.

Anna is actually described as a 'prophetess'. She had been a widow for many years, and lived all the time in the temple, worshipping, fasting and praying. She too, through her gift of prophecy, recognized the child as the Messiah, who would redeem Jerusalem.

Jesus Christ was to say some strong things against the formal religion of the Pharisees. But here were two very religious people, who spent a lot of time in formal worship, yet who, when it came to it, recognized Jesus as the Son of God.


## 4 The theophany at the Jordan

Luke 3:21–23a

Western and Eastern Christians use different words to describe the festival which immediately follows Christmas. In the West it is called 'Epiphany', and stresses the coming of the wise men to visit Christ, to inaugurate, as it were, the mission to the Gentiles. Eastern Christians call the same festival 'Theophany', and instead focus on the baptism of Christ in the River Jordan by John the Baptist. The word 'theophany' means 'manifestation of God'. The Eastern Church has always seen this occasion as especially important because it witnesses to the first manifestation recorded in the Gospels of the Holy Trinity, Father, Son and Holy Spirit. The Father speaks from heaven, the Son is baptized, and the Holy Spirit comes upon him as a dove.

One of the dominant themes of this story is the humility of the two main characters, Jesus Christ and John the Baptist. John in Matthew's account tried to deter Christ with the words, 'I need to be baptized by you, and do you come to me?' (3:13). He had also expressed his unworthiness with the words 'his sandals I am not fit to carry' (3:11). But Christ's humility was even greater. Remember he was coming to a spot where thousands were being baptized by John repenting of their sins. Christ had committed no sin. Yet he allows John to baptize him. We always need to hold together the glory and the humility of Christ, which St Augustine called the Christus humilis.

The early church always saw the baptism of Christ as the model for Christian baptism. Thus people were baptized in the name of the Trinity, and the Holy Spirit as well as the Word of God had an important part to play. We need to remember that John differentiated between his baptism which was 'unto repentance' and that of Christ which was 'with the Holy Spirit' (Matthew 3:11). During the last century one of the most influential movements has been the Pentecostal. It began at the start of the twentieth century and its main focus is on Christ, as the 'baptizer in the Holy Spirit'. Thus Christians are encouraged to seek the baptism in the Holy Spirit. Opinions will vary as to the legitimacy of their teaching, but this passage does underline the importance of the experience of the Holy Spirit in baptism.

# 5 A desert experience

Luke 4:1–13

The baptism was a breathtaking event in the life of Christ, but there follows a time of deep trial. Great moments in all our lives are often followed by similar temptations. The devil has not changed his strategy! It is important to notice that Luke tells us it was not Satan who drew him into this desert warfare, but the

Holy Spirit (v. 1), who had just come peacefully upon him in the form of a dove. We need also to notice that Jesus goes there, 'full of the Holy Spirit'. So nothing, least of all temptation, happens outside the sphere of the Holy Spirit's actions. He is always there first. And he is always the source of our power and wisdom to overcome the subtle attacks of Satan.

There is a striking contrast between this passage and the one we looked at yesterday. On the banks of the River Jordan, Christ was surrounded by large crowds of people. He was with a member of his family, John the Baptist. He also heard the reassuring voice of God the Father, and felt the touch of the Holy Spirit and his power. Now it was all different. He was whisked away to the dry unwelcoming desert by the same Holy Spirit— far from people and the refreshing river. Now he had to listen to the tempting voice of the devil.

Rivers and deserts have their place in our Christian lives. Christ spoke about the 'streams of living water' which would flow from our innermost beings (John 7:37). But the early church had also to make the most of the desert as well, and indeed as Christ did, change it into a place of blessing. It is significant that the so-called Desert Fathers, such as St Anthony, pioneered monasticism, which was to become a vital part of the life of both Eastern and Western Christianity. We too need both. Alongside the experience of being with people, we also need a 'desert experience'—of being alone with God.

It is important for us to notice that Christ fasted during this period of 40 days. Fasting was clearly taught by Christ, and has always held a place in the lives of Christians, alongside prayer and giving to the poor. The 40-day fast of Lent was a later development, and is mentioned in the Council of Nicea (AD325), becoming general by the seventh century. Should not fasting have a regular place in our lives?

# 6 Going public

Luke 4:14–15

When a person is ordained to the ministry the usual practice is to have a pre-ordination retreat, followed immediately by public service. In my day the tradition was for the new minister to preach at the service on the evening after the ordination. All that is good. But in the case of Christ it was the other way round! His 'retreat' in the desert came after his 'ordination' at the River Jordan, and his first public ministry came after that.

Notice that Luke yet again is concerned to highlight the Holy Spirit. Jesus, he tells us, 'returned to Galilee in the power of the Holy Spirit'. And we notice his becoming 'famous' overnight was due to this. We are told news about him spread fast everywhere. He was also invited to speak in the synagogues—without any formal training, or backing from influential people. His authority was divine not human, his fame came from his immersion in the Spirit, rather than in the affairs of the world. He needed no 'spin' to carry weight. We are also told that 'everyone praised him'. His popularity was instant and universal.

For a young man of 30 this was an astonishing start to a public career. When one considers that most of his life up to that point had been comparatively sheltered, it is all the more amazing. Moreover he had had no higher education, yet was immediately accepted in the synagogues, albeit in the rural areas rather than the cities.

Perhaps one of the goals of our life should be to allow the Holy Spirit alone to be our publicity manager. Someone once said, 'Never defend yourself'. One could add, 'Never promote yourself'. This means adopting an unselfconscious approach to life, and also leaving God to do any justifying that we might deem important.

## Guidelines

Christians normally address their prayers either to the Father (as in the Lord's Prayer) or to the Son (as in the Jesus Prayer). There is only one well-known prayer to the Holy Spirit, and it is used at the start of the Orthodox Eucharist, as well as in the famous Trisagion prayers. On the Monday of the Holy Spirit, the day after Pentecost Sunday, worshippers pray it on their knees, an unusual posture for them because prayers are normally said standing. As we move into the second week of our studies let us also pray this prayer on our knees.

*O heavenly King, Comforter, the Spirit of truth, who art everywhere present and fillest all things, Treasury of good things and Giver of life: Come, and abide in us, and cleanse us from every stain, and save our souls, O good One.*

# 1 Anointed lips

Luke 4:16–21

This is Jesus' first reported sermon. It was delivered in his home town, where he was well known. On the Sabbath he did what he had always done: he went to the synagogue. We are told that it 'was his custom'. From the Acts of the Apostles, Luke's other book, we know that it was customary to invite distinguished visitors to speak. No doubt news had reached the synagogue members ahead of time, and he had been praised by everyone. People would have been especially interested to hear someone from their own community who had become so famous, and so quickly.

It is probable by this time that teaching would have taken precedence over worship in the synagogue. Standing was normal for reading the Word. Although the scroll of Isaiah was handed to him (fortuitously), it would seem that Christ chose the passage he wanted to read. He would have known this famous passage, and was already seeing how he was himself fulfilling it. His sense of vocation, so strongly underlined at his baptism, was clear.

But what makes this passage all the more fascinating is that it speaks of the Holy Spirit being on him, of the spiritual anointing to preach good news. Again we see Luke drawing our attention to the ministry of the Holy Spirit, in this case in the reading of the Word. Christ sees his ministry (declared here by Isaiah) to be to the underprivileged and marginalized—the poor, the sick and the oppressed. It was already unfolding, but it was the ministry of a suffering servant.

There was a dramatic ending to the reading. 'Today,' Jesus said, 'this scripture is fulfilled in your hearing'. By using the word 'today' he revealed to the people in the synagogue that here was a word from God which was contemporary, down to earth, and coming true at that very moment. Have there been times in our lives when this has happened to us—when a passage of scripture, perhaps one with which we are very familiar, comes true in a special way in a specific moment of time? That is the work of the Holy Spirit—to make real for us what is written. He helps us to realize at times, 'this was written specially for me', or 'for this very moment'.

# 2 The Light that nothing can eclipse

Luke 9:28–36

At first sight this is a strange event, coming suddenly without apparent meaning or purpose. But one would be wrong to leave it there. It becomes for us highly significant as we look closer. We have to remember that symbolism has a big part to play in our faith, and in our worship. Clearly there are immediate parallels in the Old Testament—Moses receiving the Law on Mount Sinai, and Elijah defeating the prophets of Baal on Mount Carmel. It is not known exactly what this mountain was. Some think it is Mount Tabor, but it could have been Carmel. It is Moses and Elijah, themselves symbols of the Law and the Prophets, who appear with Christ on the mountain.

We noted that Christ's baptism was a 'theophany'. So was this occasion. The first one came at the beginning of Christ's ministry, and the second near the end when he is speaking more and more about his forthcoming death. It is Luke who tells us the subject of his conversation with these two great men: 'they talked about his departure, which he was about to bring to fulfilment in Jerusalem.' (v. 31). As at his baptism, there is the divine voice, 'This is My Son, whom I have chosen; listen to him' (v. 35). There is also the cloud which enveloped them, just as Moses experienced on Sinai, a symbolic happening of the Holy Spirit, who, as we observed earlier, overshadowed the Virgin Mary when she conceived (1:35).

On 11 August 1999 part of the United Kingdom experienced the total eclipse of the sun. It was a very rare occurrence. But God's Light, his uncreated Essence, can never be eclipsed even for a fraction of a second. In the two great feasts of Pentecost and Transfiguration light figures prominently. At Pentecost the apostles and others (including the Virgin Mary) saw tongues of fire on each of them. No one saw his own fire, only the fire of others. At the Transfiguration the appearance of the face of Christ changed, and 'his clothes became as bright as a flash of lightning' (Luke 9:29). It is also described in terms of 'glory'— 'they saw his glory', we are told.

We owe it to St Gregory Palamas to understand the important distinction between light as 'essence' and as 'energy'. God's light, part of his essence, cannot be seen by humans. But the light of God as 'energy' can be seen and experienced. In fact the apostle Paul teaches clearly that it should be part of our lives. In 2 Corinthians 3:18 he writes, 'we, who with unveiled faces all reflect the Lord's glory, are being transformed into his likeness with ever-increasing glory, which comes from the Lord, who is the Spirit.' Such is the birthright of every child of God.

## 3 Joy in mission

Luke 10:1–21

Mission is central to Christianity. It is seen supremely in the mission of the Son, sent by the Father, and anointed at his baptism by the Holy Spirit. In this account of the mission of the seventy, when they returned Christ cries out, 'I saw Satan fall like lightning from heaven' (v. 18). Very dramatic words! Surely somewhat exaggerated about a mission that could only have had a marginal impact on the area they had covered! In Luke 9 we are told about the mission of the Twelve. Apparently little drama then. What was the difference?

The answer lies in the fact that this was the first lay mission of the Church, and the future advance of Christianity was to depend so much on the laity—as well as on the ministers or priests. Satan trembles and falls when the Holy Spirit mobilizes the laity for action.

But the other note struck by this passage is 'joy'. The missioners were excited about what had happened: 'even the demons submit to us in your name!' they said (v. 17). But even their joy is eclipsed by Christ's (v. 21). The Greek word in the text is a colourful one, and 'rejoice' is not strong enough to convey its full meaning. It means a positive exultation, which may well have been expressed physically with leaping, hand waving, and shouting. Mission can be very exciting.

Luke, true to one of the major themes of his Gospel, tells us the source of this joy—the Holy Spirit (v. 21). Paul was to list joy as part of the fruit of the Holy Spirit (Galatians 5:22), coming immediately after 'love'. It is part of our heritage in the Holy Spirit and does not depend on favourable human circumstances. It flows at all times, but as here, it is especially and abundantly present, when the mission of Christ is being extended.

# 4 Praying in the Spirit

Luke 11:1–13

Christ often provoked others to imitate him. Here was an occasion when he was praying, and the disciples were so inspired by what they saw and heard that one of them asked him 'teach us to pray…' (v. 1). Jesus then taught them the most famous prayer in the world—the so-called 'Lord's Prayer'. And what a simple prayer! Prayer as Christ and the early church taught it is not complex. I suppose the second most famous prayer in the world is the 'Jesus Prayer', which comes from the tradition of the Orthodox Church, but is now used by Christians from many traditions. You can't have anything more simple and basic than the words, 'Jesus Christ, Son of God, have mercy on me'.

Jesus goes on to teach about prayer by using two parables. In the first a person arrives late at night and wants food and lodging. His friend has nothing, so he goes to another friend to beg or borrow food for his hungry visitor. Although it is very late he is prevailed upon to get up and provide the food that is so needed. Jesus says that the main reason he does it is not because of his friendship, but because of the man's desire not to bring the shame of refusing hospitality upon himself and his fellow citizens. (Here 'boldness' (v. 8) is an inadequate translation.) Thus Christ teaches that part of prayer is having confidence not to take 'no' for an answer, because God is a God of honour.

The second parable is about a father and a family. This time it is a son, who is hungry and asks for food from his father. Jesus has taught about God's faithfulness in answering prayer, and the need to trust him in prayer. But this time he underlines the goodness of God, who is like a father who 'knows how to give good gifts' to his children (v. 13). If his son asks for fish he won't be given a snake, and so on. We can utterly trust God to give us only what is good for us. He won't give us anything that bites like a snake or stings like a scorpion. When we ask, we need not worry about receiving something that will harm us.

But in this passage there is a surprise in the final words. Whereas Matthew in his Gospel records the words 'good things' to refer to what our heavenly Father gives, Luke says 'the Holy Spirit'. Jesus is teaching his disciples that they would receive the Holy Spirit through prayer, which is exactly what did happen on the Day of Pentecost—they were in prayer when the Holy Spirit came. In all this it is 'like Master, like disciple'—for it is Luke who also tells us that when Jesus received the Holy Spirit at his baptism, it was 'as he was praying' (3:21).

So Jesus teaches us by word and example that to pray properly is to 'pray in the Holy Spirit', as St Paul puts it in Ephesians 6:18. Yes, we need boldness to hold on to the faithfulness of God. We need confidence that God will only do good to us, and we need to trust the Holy Spirit to guide and inspire us in prayer.

## 5 Power to witness

Luke 12:8–12

We have already seen the way mission is vitally linked with the ministry of the Holy Spirit. In this passage we see this again. Inevitably mission involves speaking. It is true that our example, the way we live our lives, does need to match what we believe, and what we say; but this cannot take the place of clear and humble words about Christ and his kingdom.

In this passage Christ is teaching about witnessing or acknowledging him before people. He warns us about the sin of 'disowning' him. He goes on to warn about the danger of 'blaspheming against the Holy Spirit'. Christ is not here referring to swearing or taking God's name in vain. These come under the category of 'a word against the Son of Man', and Christ says that such sins 'will be forgiven' (v. 10). Blaspheming against the Holy Spirit is calling black white, and white black. Leon Morris describes it as 'the set of the life. It is so serious because it concerns the whole man, not a few words spoken on any one occasion' (Luke, Inter Varsity Press, p. 211).

Jesus then prepares the disciples for what was to become part and parcel of being Christian—persecution. It was to be common throughout the first three centuries, and has been even more common in the century that has just ended. Research would indicate that more Christians died for their faith in the twentieth century than in the whole of previous church history. Again Christ talks about the inspiration of the Holy Spirit. When we are on trial for our faith we do not have to worry about what we are going to say. The Spirit will put the words into our mouths, and at exactly the right moment. Most comforting, but not a recipe for preaching or teaching! That is a different situation, and needs careful preparation.

## 6 I am going to send

Luke 24:36–49

The presence of Christ heralds peace to his people. John records the same word 'peace' in his account of the Resurrection appearance of the Saviour. The reaction of the disciples was hardly one of faith! They were 'startled and frightened'. Clearly they were not predisposed to believing that Christ had been raised from the dead, and all the implications that involved. They thought they were seeing ghosts! Even when he had shown them his hands and his feet, with the tell-tale prints in them, they still did not believe, though this time they were overcome by joy and amazement. Hardly the kind of leaders who would turn the world upside down!

Now Christ gives them the ability to understand the scriptures, in a moment in time. It can happen to us too. There are memorable moments when the scriptures come alive. Suddenly we are aware of hidden truth. All this in a flash of inspiration. It was the same with the disciples on the road to Emmaus, which Luke records earlier in this chapter (vv. 13–35). Such disclosures are the work of the Holy Spirit, and the disciples were getting a foretaste of the coming Pentecost.

Then Jesus feeds them, and teaches them. He now tells them what they are to do. Their mission is to start at Jerusalem, and they are to spread the gospel from there to all nations. Then comes the punch-line of the whole Gospel: 'I am going to send you what the Father has promised; but stay in the city until you have been clothed with power from on high.' We have already seen what the Holy Spirit did in the lives of John the Baptist, the Virgin Mary, Elizabeth, Simeon, Anna and increasingly in the ministry of the disciples. It was all now coming to a head, and they were to receive this full blessing of Pentecost.

Like the disciples we have meagre human resources. In spite of the fact we have two thousand years of Christian history behind us, we still have not completed the great missionary task outlined here by Christ. We do have better human resources. We have radio and television, we have mass-produced books, we have videos and cassette tapes and we have the internet revolution, making information available on an ever-increasing scale. But it is no easier today than it was then to bring the nations to Christ. We need the same Holy Spirit that Christ poured out on the church at Pentecost.

## Guidelines

Sadly there has been a great deal of controversy among Christians concerning the Eucharist. But one interesting and important point of convergence is in what is called the Epiclesis, a prayer for the coming of the Holy Spirit during the consecration. This prayer has always been part of the Orthodox prayer of consecration (the Anaphora), but in recent years it has been included in some Western Eucharists. Now it is important to notice that the prayer in the original tradition includes the people as well as the bread and the wine.

*We pray Thee, and supplicate Thee: Send down thy Holy Spirit upon us and upon these gifts here spread forth…*

Views will differ about what happens at that moment, but we can and should agree that we need to pray constantly that the Holy Spirit will come upon us, as he did upon Moses, Elijah, John the Baptist, Zechariah, Elizabeth, Mary, Simeon, Anna and countless disciples of Christ. But in full measure on the Son of God.

---

**FOR FURTHER READING**

*Praying the Jesus Prayer Together*, Brother Ramon and Simon Barrington-Ward, BRF, 2001

*Living and Praying the Lord's Prayer*, Peter Graves, BRF, 2002

# DAY BY DAY
# WITH GOD

## Bible Readings for Women

*Day by Day with God* (published jointly with Christina Press) is written especially by women for women, with a regular team of contributors. Each four-monthly issue offers daily Bible readings, with key verses printed out, helpful comment and a prayer for the day ahead. Our readings in this sampler, on the theme 'In God's hands', come from Jennifer Rees Larcombe, one of Britain's best-loved Christian authors and speakers. She is the author of *Beauty from Ashes* (BRF, 2000).

# Creative hands

*Come, let us sing for joy to the Lord… In his hand are the depths of the earth, and the mountain peaks belong to him. The sea is his, for he made it and his hands formed the dry ground. (Psalm 95:5)*

*In his hand is the life of every creature and the breath of all mankind. (Job 12:10)*

*Your hands shaped me and made me… Remember that you moulded me like clay. (Job 10:8–9)*

I am writing this on a secluded beach in Devon. Getting here involves a long hike and a risky climb down the cliffs, so there are no ice-cream kiosks, deck chairs or beach huts; absolutely everything I can see was made by God himself. I could probably count a million of them if I had powerful binoculars and a microscope. Gulls soar over the towering cliffs behind me, gigantic cumulous clouds drift overhead and the sea sucks gently round the rocks. I've spent the afternoon enjoying the rock pools, fascinated by all the different colours of the seaweed, anemones and the tiny darting fish. Even the little stones between my toes all have their individual shapes.

So few ever come here that all this staggering beauty exists almost exclusively for God's pleasure. Why not, his hands made it— but does the Almighty have hands? Did he roll the earth into a ball in his palms and fling it into orbit? Well the Bible tells us he not only has palms but our names are tattooed on them (Isaiah 49:16). David, the shepherd, tells us it was God's fingers that made the moon and the stars (Psalm 8:3). And God himself says, 'My own hands stretched out the heavens' (Isaiah 45:12). God is so powerful that he can create anything merely by a word of command, but perhaps he uses the word hands because he longs to make it easier for us to identify with him.

---

*Thank you, Father, that you have the whole world in your hand.*

*'Father, into your hands I commit my spirit' (Luke 23:46).*

*Psalm 44:1–8 (NIV)*

# Loving hands

*It was not by their sword that they won the land, nor did their arm bring them victory; it was your right hand, your arm, and the light of your face, for you loved them.*

Recently I sat holding my mother-in-law's hand as she peacefully slept her way into heaven. As I thought about those hands, now so still but in the past so constantly active, I wondered how many acts of love they had performed during their 86 years: caring for her disabled mother, feeding, washing and changing her three babies—and my six! All those birthday cakes they had decorated; delicious puddings that ruined all my diets; mountains of ironing and washing-up they had worked through and the many grazed knees and elbows they had tended. She was always shy about expressing her love in words, but her hands said it all!

Hands are so expressive that it is not surprising people in Old Testament days often linked God's hands with his love and care. Ezra the priest did it often when he wrote his astonishing account of how he led thousands of Jewish captives back to their homeland over a bandit-infested desert.

'The king had granted him everything he asked, for the hand of the Lord his God was on him' (Ezra 7:6). 'I was ashamed to ask the king for soldiers and horsemen to protect us from enemies on the road, because we had told the king, "The gracious hand of our God is on everyone who looks to him…" So we fasted and petitioned our God about this, and he answered our prayer' (Ezra 8:22–24). 'Because the hand of the Lord my God was on me, I took courage' (Ezra 7:28). 'On the twelfth day of the first month we set out… to go to Jerusalem. The hand of our God was on us, and he protected us from enemies and bandits along the way' (Ezra 8:31).

---

*Lord, thank you that you promise to cover me, today, with the shadow of your hand (Isaiah 51:16).*

# Overshadowing hand

**The Holy Spirit will come upon you, and the power of the
Most High will overshadow you.**

Perhaps the phrase 'the hand of the Lord' means something
different to each of us. Certainly this was so for two Bible contributors who both used the term often. For Ezra, having God's hand
with him meant guidance and protection, but for Ezekiel, it meant
something totally different. He lived in Babylon, where he and his
fellow Jews had been dragged as captives after their nation's defeat.
They were living in isolated ghettos all over the vast empire. Ezekiel
was an itinerant prophet, travelling constantly between the groups,
teaching and encouraging. As he wrote his book, he looked back
over many years of ministry, but certain moments stood out vividly.
They were times when he felt God's presence so strongly that he
often fell to the ground. They were so important to him that he
recorded the date and described exactly where he was (by the Kebar
River, in the village of Tel Abib, or in his own home).

Obviously Ezekiel felt that the Holy Spirit was overshadowing
him like a giant hand as he heard God speak and was shown
prophetic pictures. Modern psychologists would describe this as an
altered state of consciousness and theologians might say he was 'slain
in the Spirit'! But for Ezekiel they were the vital milestones in his life.

Can you remember times when you felt God came very close to
you?

We do not know how it felt for Mary, when the 'the power of
the Most High overshadowed her', but something supernatural
happened, for God himself began to grow inside her. Something is
planted in us, too, when God comes to us in those private and special
moments, whether we fall to the ground dramatically, like Ezekiel, or
simply feel a supernatural calm in the middle of one of life's storms.

---

*Could you make a list of your own 'God encounters'? Note where
they happened, what you felt like, who else was involved and how
they changed you.*

*Isaiah 41:1–13 (NIV)*

# Holding hands

*For I am the Lord, your God, who takes hold of your right hand and says to you, 'Do not fear; I will help you.'*

We shake hands to express friendship, to 'make up', or to cement a business deal—and what about the thrill of holding hands with someone you love? Obviously hands are a very important part of relationships.

Some of the children I used to foster had been so badly treated that they found it very hard to trust adults. One small boy had been regularly tied into his bed for 16 hours at a stretch. His body was covered with bruises and festering sores and the way he cowered away, when I tried to touch him, was heartbreaking. I don't think he had ever seen the sea, so when we took all the children for a day on the beach he became rigid with terror at the sight of the waves rolling towards him. Suddenly a cold, clammy hand was thrust into mine. All day he clutched my hand tenaciously, refusing to let it go even if that meant eating his precious packet of crisps with his left hand!

By the afternoon, his confidence had grown enough to allow him to run with me through the sandy puddles left by the retreating tide. His little legs had never been given the chance to run and jump before, so he often stumbled. 'You won't let me fall, will you?' he would say anxiously. 'Keep hold of my hand—promise?'

That day changed him. Gradually he became a normal, happy child, but it was the action of grabbing my hand that began our relationship. God's top priority with us is our relationship with him. He longs for us to grab his hand like that, whenever we feel afraid, lonely or confused.

---

*'My soul clings to you; your right hand upholds me' (Psalm 63:8).*

*'If the Lord delights in a man's way, he makes his steps firm; though he stumble, he will not fall, for the Lord upholds him with his hand' (Psalm 37:23).*

# Warning hands

### The Lord's hand has gone out against me!

Suddenly, round the corner, a policeman appeared holding up his hand. As I jammed on my brakes, he shouted, 'There's been an accident, you'll have to go back.'

While we all enjoy the comforting verses about God's hands protecting and guiding us, there are also many that describe his 'hand against' individuals or nations. Sometimes God says, 'If you don't get out of this relationship... stop this habit... this activity... you'll be in danger of losing your integrity... your spiritual health... people you love.' We can then choose to stop, or go on regardless of the consequences. There are also several references to God's hand being heavy, rather as a father's hand might feel heavy to his disobedient offspring!

When we ignore God's hand of warning, and allow some temptation to become a way of life, his punishment does not always fall in this life. God's grace is so enormous that he gives us time for repentance, but these days we are dangerously inclined to think that God is *all* love and *only* love. He *is* love, of course, but he is also righteousness. He cannot overlook sin, because it hurts innocent people: justice has to be done, so every sin we ever commit has to be punished, ultimately. When we repent, Jesus himself takes that punishment for us, but there are Christians who find a particular sin so attractive that they prefer to continue in it, rather than repent and change. The sin robs them of God's favour and blessing that they once enjoyed, but they refuse to recognize consequences such as guilt and loss of peace as 'God's heavy hand' on them. The book of Hebrews says some very serious things about Christians like this.

---

'If we deliberately keep on sinning after we have received the knowledge of the truth, no sacrifice for sins is left... The Lord will judge his people. It is a dreadful thing to fall into the hands of the living God' (Hebrews 10:26, 30–31).

Is there a 'danger area' in your life?

# Appreciative hands

*You will be a crown of splendour in the Lord's hand, a royal diadem in the hand of your God.*

Crowns are usually associated with heads rather than hands! But as I turned this verse over in my mind, I realized that you can't see a crown if you are wearing it. You have to hold it in your hands to enjoy it to the full. You need to feel the smoothness of the gold, and turn the jewels in the light to see them sparkle. Most of us have such horribly low self-esteem that the idea of God gaining pleasure from looking at us feels bizarre! We often develop a low opinion of ourselves in childhood. Adults called us stupid, clumsy, bad or difficult, and we grew up labelled by these invisible names. In Isaiah 62:2, God promises to change our name (that is, our identity). He is in the business of changing people, and goes on to say in verse 4, 'No longer will they call you Deserted, or… Desolate. But you will be called Hephzibah (The Lord is delighted with you).'

We *can* think differently about ourselves when we see how *God* thinks about us!

So what great things do we have to achieve in order to become this treasure that the Lord holds so proudly? It is not a question of what we do but how we react to what others do. Pearls are formed when a grain of sand gets into the oyster's shell, irritating its soft body until it wraps the sand round with the protective layers which, later, form a valuable jewel. Diamonds are created only after years of pressure. Gold has to be exposed to intense heat so that all the impurities surface and can be skimmed off (see Job 23:10). Accepting, without bitterness, the heat of life's traumas, grinding pressures or endless small irritations is what forms, what God calls our 'treasures of darkness' (Isaiah 45:3).

---

*Lord, help me to realize that all these problems that weigh me down can be transformed by you into something beautiful which will one day give you great delight.*

*Psalm 139:7–12 (NIV)*

# Guiding hands

*If I make my bed in the depths, you are there… if I settle on
the far side of the sea, even there your hand will guide me, your
right hand will hold me fast. If I say, 'Surely the darkness will
hide me and the light become night around me', even the darkness
will not be dark to you; the night will shine like the day,
for darkness is as light to you.*

Life can sometimes feel frighteningly dark, can't it? We feel lost and
not sure which way to turn. David, who wrote this psalm, felt like
this often, but he assures us that God's hand was always there to
guide him through frightening or confusing situations. Our foster
daughter, Jane, was seven when she came to us. Her father had died
suddenly that day; she had lost her mother through cancer a couple
of years previously.

At first she settled quite well, but then the panic attacks began.
The first one literally paralysed her with fright during a school
firework party, but soon they happened anywhere.

One day I took her shopping. She was chattering happily as we
walked along the crowded pavement together, when a car backfired
behind her and triggered an attack. This time she was not rooted to
the spot: she ran wildly, heading straight for the busy road, blinded
by terror. Diving after her, I caught her—just in time. She did not
respond to my comforting words: I had to take her somewhere safe,
but she was too big to carry. So, holding her unwilling hand very
tightly, I guided her rapidly between the crowds of shoppers in the
direction of the park. There, on a bench, I rocked her in my arms
until she was peaceful again.

I know, now, how horrible panic attacks feel, when life suddenly
loses all its landmarks, familiar structures and special people, leaving
you feeling lost and confused. But God's guiding hand is there, and
he won't let us take a wrong turn.

---

*Please hold my hand today, Lord.*

*Isaiah 65:1–5 (NIV)*

# Rejected hands

*All day long I have held out my hands to an obstinate people,*
*who walk in ways not good, pursuing their own imaginations—*
*a people who continually provoke me to my very face.*

Our friendly church was being changed into a battleground by a
violent disagreement. Friends were transformed into enemies overnight and the pain we were inflicting on each other was staggering.
Matters were coming to a messy head in the church meeting. I sat
in tears as I looked round the room, loving people on both sides.
Suddenly, I lost my cool and, standing up, I told them all to stop
behaving like spoilt children and breaking our Father's heart!

The following Sunday I was on 'welcome duty' at the church
door, which meant shaking hands with everyone. I stood there with
my welcoming smile and my hand held out, but, one by one, people
from both sides walked past me, ignoring my hand. I had probably
asked for it by being tactless, but these were old friends, some of
whom I'd led to the Lord, and others were members of my own
house-group. It all blew over in a few weeks, but every time I read
the verse at the top of this page, I remember the agony I felt that
morning.

The more we love someone, the greater is their capacity to hurt
us by their rejection, so God must feel infinitely worse than I can
imagine when so many of the people for whom he died ignore him
completely.

---

*Lord I know you hold your hands out to me, too, all day long. I almost
hear you say, 'Come and sit with me a while,' but I switch on TV. 'Tell
me how you're feeling, share this worry with me,' but I ring a friend.
'Why don't you ask for my help?' But I stress myself out, trying to
solve the problem myself. 'Come and let me hold you,' but I open a
packet of biscuits for comfort. Please forgive me for ignoring your
outstretched hands so often.*

# Jesus' hands

*As the eyes of slaves look to the hand of their master...*
*so our eyes look to the Lord our God.*

During the last few days we've been looking at some of the references to God's hands in the Old Testament. Perhaps they have seemed rather abstract, but we can all identify with the hands of Jesus and it is by watching them that we learn most about the character of God.

We only have our imaginations to go on for his first thirty years, and many delightful but fictitious stories are told about the way his childish hands mended birds' wings or broken toys. However, we are given a generous list of things his hands actually did during his last three years. Not only did he lay them on the sick but he wrote in the dust, washed feet, served meals and even cooked a beach barbeque.

His hands must have been strong, skilful, suntanned and roughened by years of manual work. They were also incredibly gentle and tender. Mark remembers how Jesus used a child as an illustration for his quarrelling disciples. He didn't just point him out to them from a safe, adult distance: 'He took a little child (by the hand) and had him stand among them. Taking him in his arms, he said to them, "Whoever welcomes one of these little children in my name welcomes me"' (Mark 9:36).

Mark also tells us how Jesus bent down and lifted a child to his feet after an epileptic fit. The child's father was there so Jesus could easily have left him to care for his son, who had been writhing on the filthy ground in his own dribble, urine and, possibly, vomit. Instead, Jesus himself reached down to restore his dignity, perhaps wiped the little boy's mouth and smoothed the sweaty hair from his bewildered eyes, before taking his hand and lifting him up.

---

*Thank you that you don't expect me to clean myself up when I've been on the ground. Your hands reach down to me in the mess where I am.*

# Dirty hands

*Filled with compassion, Jesus reached out his hand and touched
the man. 'I am willing,' he said. 'Be clean!'*

It amazes me to realize how willing Jesus was to get his hands dirty.
This is particularly remarkable in days when people who were
considered holy washed their hands repeatedly throughout the day
(Mark 7:1–6) and wouldn't even permit the shadow of a prostitute
to fall on their path. They held their cloaks tightly when they walked
through a crowd in case they brushed someone who was 'unclean'—
the disabled; those with skin diseases or discharges; lepers and
menstruating women. Yet Jesus, who had the power to heal by
'remote control', often touched people like that.

He was nearing a village one day when he met a funeral pro-
cession. In the middle of the crowd of wailing women, one face
looked so agonized that 'his heart went out to her' (Luke 7:13). She
was the mother of the young man who had just died, and he was all
she had left in the world.

'Don't cry,' said Jesus softly. He could have raised the corpse with
a word, like he did for Lazarus; instead he put his hand on the coffin
and the bearers stopped amazed, because touching a corpse also
made you unclean.

Jesus is not high above the ugliness of grief; he's right there in the
centre of it.

Another time his path was blocked by the grotesque figure of a
kneeling leper. The disease causes the flesh of its victims to be eaten
away, leaving them covered with infectious and disfiguring sores.
'You could help me, if you wanted to,' the man said. Because lepers
were outcasts, considered lowest of the low without status or rights,
maybe he didn't feel the kind of person Jesus would bother to help.
The hand of Jesus was the first that had touched him in years! (Luke
5:12–13).

---

*Lord, sometimes I, also, feel I'm not 'quite the right sort of person' for
you to want to help. When I think like that, help me to remember how
you touched that leper.*

Psalm 145:8–18 (NIV)

# Generous hands

*You open your hand and satisfy the desires of every living thing.*

Jesus often used his hands to give. The one who had voluntarily given up ownership of the entire universe had no money or possessions to share, but when a small boy gave him his picnic lunch Jesus immediately gave it away to the hungry people surrounding him (John 6:9–13). His hands multiplied his own personal supply of food like that on a number of occasions.

The only other thing Jesus could give was his blessing. When mothers eagerly approached him, longing for him to pray for their children, the disciples rudely shooed them away. Mark tells us, 'Jesus was indignant, 'And he took the children in his arms, put his hands on them and blessed them' (Mark 10:16). Don't we all long to see his hands touching our own children like that!

On the first Easter Sunday evening, a couple asked him to supper. Because they were traumatized by the crucifixion, they did not recognize him until he stretched out his hand to give them a piece of bread during the simple meal. The nails had left that hand so horribly bruised and distorted that they recognized him instantly (Luke 24:30–31). That story always moves me to tears, and so does this one: the host at a Jewish festival meal used to dip a piece of bread in the sauce and hand it to the guest he honoured most highly. Just minutes after Jesus had used his hands to wash the feet of Judas Iscariot, he also handed him this special 'sop'. He already knew what Judas planned to do that night, so was he offering him one last chance to save himself from being labelled as the worst traitor in history? (John 13:18–30).

---

*Could you stop for a moment and picture those wounded hands reaching out to you? Ask him what they are offering you: a chance to change; the opportunity to know him better; blessings for your family; some new spiritual gift or anointing for service; the daily bread— ordinary necessities—that you need today?*

# Restoring hands

*So he went to her, took her hand and helped her up. The fever left her and she began to wait on them.*

I can remember lying in bed fuming during my eight years of illness, when I often had to listen helplessly to my husband and children creating chaos in the kitchen below. Illness, disability, loss and old age rapidly sap our confidence, making us feel marginalized. Was this how Peter's mum-in-law felt, the day a very special visitor came for a meal? One touch of his hand and she was up, dressed and busy in the kitchen! Jesus does not always restore health, youth or mobility but his touch always restores hope and gives us a reason for living. His servants are never on 'the sick list' and never retired. Serving him may not mean doing the active, practical jobs, but the words 'worship' and 'serve' are the same in Hebrew. Do you need his hand to restore your ability to enjoy his company and intercede for others?

Who else but Peter would have jumped out of a boat on a stormy night, walked a few steps on the water, and then panicked! Matthew says he yelled, 'Lord, save me!' Immediately Jesus reached out his hand and caught him (Matthew 14:30–31). Have you ever felt you were drowning in problems, worries and confusion? Peter was never safer than at the moment when he felt most afraid, because it was then that Jesus reached out to hold him. It was merely Peter's faith that needed restoring.

The hand of Jesus can also restore life. When an agitated father hurried Jesus through the crowds to his daughter, who had just died, Jesus took her hand, and she lived! (Mark 5:41).

---

*Is there an area of your life that has died—your faith, hope or creativity; the love or respect you once had for a husband, parent or child? Has your joy died, killed by despair? Has your peace been strangled by worry? Could Jesus be holding out his hand to you, longing to restore life to that dead place?*

Mark 7:32–35 (NIV)

# Healing hands

*People brought to him a man who was deaf and could hardly talk,*
*and they begged him to place his hand on the man. After he took*
*him aside, away from the crowd, Jesus put his fingers into the*
*man's ears. Then he spat and touched the man's tongue. He*
*looked up to heaven and with a deep sigh said to him,*
*'Ephphatha!' (which means, 'Be opened!').*

During eight years of illness, I read all the Christian books on healing,
desperately trying to discover the secret formula that would make me
well. Some 'experts' claimed that healing comes through the laying on
of hands, while others insisted it's all down to deliverance, lengthy
prayer counselling, or being 'slain in the Spirit'. Finally I concluded that
there isn't a formula: Jesus worked differently with each individual.

Tracy finds crowds very confusing because of her deafness; often
she can't understand what is happening. I wonder if that is how the
man in today's story felt when the crowd dragged him to Jesus. They
wanted to see a miracle: how cross they must have been when Jesus
took him by the hand and walked off with him!

Jesus knew it would terrify the man if he suddenly heard the
noise of an excited crowd after hearing nothing all his life. Rather
than startle him, Jesus used his hands to communicate what he was
doing by sign language. He put his fingers in the man's ears, touched
his tongue, looked up to indicate he was praying and then spoke a
single word which would have been easy to lip-read.

I wonder what people at a healing service would think if, instead
of administering the 'laying on of hands' at the communion rail, the
vicar started spitting in their eyes and mouths!

---

*Thank you, Lord, that you treat us all as individuals. May I never try*
*to put you in a box, tied up neatly with academic ribbons and*
*theological bows. I don't understand why you heal some and not*
*others, but I know you do not require me to understand you, only to*
*trust you.*

Luke 23:33–43 (NIV)

# Helpless hands

*When they came to the place called the Skull, there they crucified him… Jesus said, 'Father, forgive them, for they do not know what they are doing.'*

We have been looking at some of the things which the Bible tells us were done by the 'hands that flung stars into space' (Graham Kendrick). Surely the most incredible of them all was their apparent helplessness when thugs nailed iron stakes right through them. How did Jesus feel as those cruel, mocking faces hovered over him and the hammer blows began? He was no longer considering escape; he had already battled out that issue in Gethsemane (Luke 22:42). Rage or fear could be expected at a time like that, but it was love that he felt, love for the men who were torturing him and love for you and me, as he allowed himself to take the punishment which should have been ours.

Was there was something that hurt even more than those hammer-blows? The helplessness he felt during the hours that followed must have been terrible. When those active, generous hands were pinned to the cross, apparently useless, he must have longed to wipe the tears from his mother's face and reach out to comfort his friend John. I guess we can all identify with that sense of helplessness as we watch our child plunging headlong into a destructive relationship or course of action—when he or she is too old to be grabbed and pulled back to safety; or the helplessness we feel as we watch the person we love dying in pain or when someone else is destroying our marriage. It is always a comfort to know that Jesus understands how we feel, but in actual fact he was *not* helpless. He *could* have stepped down from that cross, but he chose not to. We are not helpless either. Praying, which can seem so inactive, may actually be the very best way to help other people.

---

*Lord, I refuse this suffocating sense of helplessness as I watch these people I love. I choose, instead, to fight for them by prayer.*

# PBC INTRODUCTION

BRF's *People's Bible Commentary* series is planned to cover the whole Bible, with a daily readings approach that brings together both personal devotion and reflective study. Combining the latest scholarship with straightforward language and a reverent attitude to Scripture, it aims to instruct the head and warm the heart. The authors come from around the world and across the Christian traditions, and offer serious yet accessible commentary. The series is an invaluable resource for first-time students of the Bible, for all who read the Bible regularly, for study group leaders, and anyone involved in preaching and teaching Scripture. Volumes are published twice a year, and the series is scheduled for completion in 2005.

The General Editors for the series are the Revd Dr Richard A. Burridge, New Testament scholar and Dean of King's College, London; Dom Henry Wansbrough OSB, Master of St Benet's Hall, Oxford and Editor of The New Jerusalem Bible; Canon David Winter, writer, broadcaster and Consulting Editor for BRF's *New Daylight* Bible reading notes.

Our PBC extracts in this sampler are from *Romans* by James D.G. Dunn, Lightfoot Professor of Divinity in the University of Durham, and *Chronicles to Nehemiah* by Michael Tunnicliffe, Director of Studies for the Northern Ordination Course, based in Manchester.

# PBC EXTRACTS

ROMANS 8:3–4

## WHAT GOD HAS DONE IN CHRIST

Romans 8:3–4 is one of Paul's classic summaries of the gospel. It has everything—God's overall purpose and initiative; the description of the human plight; the person and work of Christ; and the intended outcome in terms of ethical living and the Spirit's enabling.

### The human plight

In the order of the Greek in which the sentence was written, it is the human plight which is spoken of first. That plight is summed up on this occasion in terms of the weakness of the flesh and the incapacity of the law to counter it effectively. 'Sin' is not mentioned immediately, but in the light of all that Paul has said in 5:12—8:2 it would have been impossible to avoid mentioning it. Thus in the following clauses it becomes clear again that the real culprit is sin (it is mentioned three times in verse 3). But for the moment it is the fatal combination of a flesh too weak to obey God's law and the law as not fitted to counter that weakness which is in view.

Chapter 8 is where Paul tackles the problem of the flesh. In Romans 6—8 he had set himself to discuss what role (if any) the fearful alliance of sin and death, with the law as their catspaw (5:20), should have in the Christian's life. That interplay of sin and death, and of sin, law and death, in human experience (not excluding that of the believer), has been his main concern in Romans 6—7, though his treatment of them is not yet completed. However, in the course of that exposition it became clear that the flesh and its weakness were a further factor in the equation (7:5, 14, 18). It is that feature on which he initially focuses here.

It is worth recalling that, for Paul, the 'flesh' denotes the frailty of the human being which ends in death, and the weakness of humankind in ever pandering to appetite and desire against humankind's best interest. This is what the law in itself was inadequate to counter; the remedy must come from within.

## God's initiative

The subject of the whole sentence is 'God'. Human weakness is such that only God can meet it. He does so in two ways.

First, he sent his Son 'in the very likeness of sinful flesh', that is, to deal with the problem from within. The implication is not that Christ himself was a sinner, but that he shared the flesh of humankind, the flesh whose weakness gave sin its opportunity (7:5). This is Paul's equivalent to Hebrews 4:15. Jesus experienced the frailty of humankind to the full; he knew in personal experience that enticement to personal advantage, for desire to become lust. The real humanity of Jesus was never in question for Paul.

Moreover, he sent Christ also 'for sin'. Since the same phrase is often used in the Greek Old Testament for 'sin offering', that is probably how the phrase here should be translated. Paul again draws on the Old Testament sacrificial system to find the best metaphor for Jesus' death (cf. 3:25). He died as the embodiment of 'sinful flesh'. And thus he (the subject is still 'God') 'condemned sin in the flesh'. In other words, the power of sin had such a hold on human flesh that there was no help for it other than destruction. God is the divine surgeon who recognizes that the cancer of sin has so eaten into the flesh of humanity that there is no salvation for humanity other than by radical surgery, by the complete destruction of that cancerous tissue. That radical surgery took place, as it were, on the cross. The humanity which emerged from the operation is free from the cancer (6:7).

## The outcome

The purpose of God's intervention is the rescue and rehabilitation of a humanity which can, after all, live in accordance with God's will (v. 4). So, in addition to sending his Son, God has sent his Spirit. Christ dealt with the weakness of the flesh, and the sin which exploited that weakness, from within the human situation. The Spirit deals with the weakness of the law from within the life of the believer. By countering the power of sin, the power of God counters the power which entrapped the 'I' and thwarted the purpose of God through the law.

## Prayer

*Thanks be to God for Christ, who shared our human weakness all the way to death and experienced the power of sin in all its enticing attractiveness, but who refused that enticement and died that we might be free.*

# THE QUEEN OF SHEBA

The visit of the famous Queen of Sheba is one of those biblical stories that has excited the imagination of poets, artists, story-tellers and film-makers down the ages. A whiff of the exotic wafts through the story like the romantic fragrance of the spices the queen brought with her.

## 'Take my breath away'

Sheba was one of the kingdoms in the far south of Arabia, modern-day Yemen. The lavish, impressive qualities of Solomon's court and entourage are breathtaking to the queen. The literal translation of the end of verse 4 is, 'There was no more breath/spirit left in her.'

The wealth of the land of Sheba came from its trade, especially in valuable spices and aromatic gums such as frankincense and myrrh. Thus the queen brings these precious gifts to Solomon, along with a large quantity of gold and jewels. It is worth comparing the sentiments in Psalm 72, a psalm which is traditionally linked to Solomon.

> May the kings of Tarshish and of the isles render him tribute,
> may the kings of Sheba and Seba bring gifts.
> May all kings fall down before him, all nations give him service...
> Long may he live! May gold of Sheba be given to him.
> (PSALM 72:10–11, 15A, NRSV)

In time, this psalm was taken to refer to the coming Messiah. Matthew's Gospel recounts the visit of the magi from the east at the birth of Jesus. Like the Queen of Sheba nearly one thousand years before, they bring gold, frankincense and myrrh to the 'king of the Jews'. Yet for the Gospel writers, 'something greater than

Solomon is here' (Matthew 12:42)—the very embodiment of Wisdom. For Matthew, the Gentile Queen of Sheba stands as a reproof against the unbelieving cities of Galilee who fail to recognize Jesus' true greatness.

## The queen's speech

In her speech to the king (vv. 5–8), the Queen of Sheba expresses her admiration and wonder. The queen praises Solomon in extravagant terms, but her speech also includes words of praise to God (v. 8). The grandeur of Solomon's court is not mere ostentation and extravagance. It is a sign of the wisdom granted him by the Lord, and above all of the love that God has for his people Israel. Like Huram before her, this Gentile visitor recognizes the hand of God behind the glory that is Solomon's.

## Fair exchange

Wherever the land of Ophir was, whether in India or Africa, Sheba would be an important trading-post *en route*. Therefore, although the Bible presents the queen's visit primarily in terms of her admiration for Solomon's wisdom, we should not preclude the possibility of commercial incentives too. The exchange of gifts might represent the fruits of these lucrative trade agreements. There was mutual benefit to be gained—access to the valuable spices and resins of the east for Solomon, and access to wider markets for the queen.

Among the specific items mentioned in verses 10 and 11 is the mysterious 'algum wood'. This has tentatively been identified with red sandalwood from India or Sri Lanka. It was clearly of a type unknown to Israel and was highly prized.

Verse 12 concludes the story of the queen's visit. The enigmatic phrase 'Solomon granted the queen of Sheba every desire' has been much debated, and popular legends have made much of it. According to ancient traditions, Solomon and the queen became lovers and the queen returned home expecting Solomon's child. In Ethiopia, the story was told that this child was Merelik I, the founder of the Ethiopian dynasty. That may well be an exotic fantasy, but it shows how one nation sought to link its 'story' with that of the Bible. British people do exactly the same with the legends of Joseph of Arimathea and the site of Glastonbury. Joseph is supposed to have brought the boy Jesus to England. This legend is commemorated in William Blake's poem, 'And did those feet in ancient time walk upon England's mountains green?' Somehow each of us would like to feel that our story connects with the biblical narrative. The story of the Queen of Sheba is one of the biblical tales that sets the imagination running in overdrive.

## Reflection

*Why do some stories excite our imaginations and become the 'stuff of legend'? Can you think of others that do the same?*

# ADVENT AND LENT

BRF's Advent and Lent books are among the highlights of our publishing year, with well-known authors choosing their own distinctive theme around which they offer daily Bible readings, comment and points for reflection or prayer for every day in Advent and Lent. Material for group use is also included. While our Advent books are published in September, before the Christmas season begins, our Lent titles appear in November so that churches can use them when planning their Lent reading for the following spring.

Recent Lent books include *When They Crucified My Lord* by Brother Ramon SSF, *Faith Odyssey* by Richard Burridge, and *With Jesus in the Upper Room* by David Winter. Among our recent Advent books are *On the Way to Bethlehem* by Hilary McDowell, *A Candle of Hope* by Garth Hewitt, and *The Heart of Christmas* by Chris Leonard.

# 'SEASONS OF LIFE'

BRF also publishes books of Bible readings for people at different stages of life or in particular circumstances, as part of our regular publishing programme of adult titles. *Never Too Old to Grow* by Alexine Crawford is a book of readings for carers, combining insights from the Bible with stories of personal change and growth, drawn from the experiences of caring for people in the final 'Fourth Age' of life. By contrast, *In the Beginning* by Stephen and Jacqui Hance offers Bible insights for the first weeks of parenting, taking passages from across Scripture and exploring the simple lessons that they teach for this challenging time of life. Among other titles in this range are *Beauty from Ashes* by Jennifer Rees Larcombe (readings for times of loss), *Summer Wisdom* by Eric Rew (reflections from the book of Proverbs) and *The Best is Yet to Be* by Richard Morgan (a book of readings for older people).

# HOW TO ORDER BRF NOTES

If you have enjoyed reading this sampler and would like to order the dated notes on a regular basis, they can be obtained through:

## CHRISTIAN BOOKSHOPS

Most Christian bookshops stock BRF notes and books. You can place a regular order with your bookshop for yourself or for your church. For details of your nearest stockist please contact the BRF office.

## INDIVIDUAL SUBSCRIPTION

### For yourself

By placing an annual subscription for BRF notes, you can ensure you will receive your copy regularly. We also send you additional information about BRF: BRF News, information about our new publications and updates about our ministry activities.

You can also order a subscription for three years (two years for *Day by Day with God*), for an even easier and more economical way to obtain your Bible reading notes.

### Gift subscription

Why not give a gift subscription to *New Daylight*, *Guidelines* or *Day by Day with God* to a friend or family member? Simply complete all parts of the order form and return it to us with your payment. You can even enclose a message for the gift recipient.

For either of the above, please complete the 'Individual Subscription Order Form' and send with your payment to BRF.

## CHURCH SUBSCRIPTION

If you order, directly from BRF, five or more copies from our Bible reading notes range of *New Daylight*, *Guidelines* or *Day by Day with God*, they will be sent post-free. This is known as a church subscription and it is a convenient way of bulk-ordering notes for your church. There is no need to send payment with your initial order. Please complete the 'Church Subscriptions Order Form' and we will send you an invoice with your first delivery of notes.

- **Annual subscription:** you can place a subscription for a full year, receiving one invoice for the year. Once you place an annual church subscription, you will be sent the requested number of Bible reading notes automatically. You will also receive useful information to help you run your church group. You can amend your order at any time, as your requirements increase or decrease. Church subscriptions run from May to April of each year. If you start in the middle of a subscription year, you will receive an invoice for the remaining issues of the current subscription year.
- **Standing order:** we can set up a standing order for your Bible reading notes order. Approximately six to seven weeks before a new edition of the notes is due to start, we will process your order and send it with an invoice.

**DAY by DAY with GOD**
BIBLE READINGS FOR WOMEN

SEPTEMBER–DECEMBER 2002

PLUS: The New Daylight Magazine
Lisa Cherrett · Rosie Parker
Katherine Dell · Gary Mayes

**New Daylight**

David Spriggs
Rob Gillion
Veronica Zundel
David Winter
Christine Chapman
Jenny Robertson
Rachel Boulding
Margaret Cundiff
Peter Graves
Rob Gillion
Adrian Plass
Jenny Robertson

on Genesis
on Matthew
on The Her
on Number
on Galatia
on The Ch
on Acts
on Gene
on Isaia
on Prop
on Acts
on Chr

**Daily readings from**

**Guidelines** IN-DEPTH BIBLE STUDY

September–December 2002

*The Ministry of Jesus*
KENNETH BAILEY

*Nahum and Obadiah*
ALEC GILMORE

*N.T. Minor Characters*
CLARE AMOS

*2 Samuel*
DONALD MURRAY

*John 7—12*
DAVID ISTE

*Readings for Advent*
HENRY WANSBROUGH

*Readings for Christmas*
JOHN PARR

Plus The Guidelines
Maxine Herbe · Lucy Moore · Rosie Parker · Ernest Lucas

# INDIVIDUAL & GIFT SUBSCRIPTIONS

This completed coupon should be sent with appropriate payment to BRF. Alternatively, please write to us quoting your name, address, the subscription you would like for either yourself or a friend (with their name and address), the start date and credit card number, expiry date and signature if paying by credit card.

☐ I would like to take out a subscription myself (complete name and address details only once)

☐ I would like to give a gift subscription (please complete both name and address sections below)

Your name _____

Your address _____

_____

_____ Postcode _____

Gift subscription name _____

Gift subscription address _____

_____

_____ Postcode _____

Please send beginning with the September / January / May issue: *(delete as applicable)*

| *(please tick box)* | **UK** | **SURFACE** | **AIR MAIL** |
|---|---|---|---|
| New Daylight | ☐ £10.50 | ☐ £11.85 | ☐ £14.10 |
| New Daylight 3-year sub | ☐ £26.50 | | |
| New Daylight LARGE PRINT | ☐ £16.20 | ☐ £19.80 | ☐ £24.30 |
| Guidelines | ☐ £10.50 | ☐ £11.85 | ☐ £14.10 |
| Guidelines 3-year sub | ☐ £26.50 | | |
| Day by Day with God | ☐ £11.55 | ☐ £12.90 | ☐ £15.15 |
| Day by Day with God 2-year sub | ☐ £19.99 | | |

Total enclosed £ _____ (cheques should be made payable to 'BRF')

Payment by ☐ cheque ☐ postal order ☐ Visa ☐ Mastercard ☐ Switch

Card number: ☐☐☐☐☐☐☐☐☐☐☐☐☐☐☐☐☐☐

Expiry date of card: ☐☐☐☐ Issue number (Switch): ☐☐☐

Signature _____ Date / /
*(essential if paying by credit/Switch card)*

Please complete the payment details above and send your coupon, with appropriate payment to: BRF, First Floor, Elsfield Hall, 15–17 Elsfield Way, Oxford OX2 8FG.

☐ Please do not mail me with other information about BRF

SAM0202 *BRF is a Registered Charity*

# CHURCH SUBSCRIPTIONS

Name _____

Address _____

_____

_____ Postcode _____

Telephone Number_____

E-mail _____

Church _____

Denomination _____

Name of Minister _____

Please start my order from Jan/May/Sep* *(delete as applicable)*

I would like to pay annually / receive an invoice each issue of the notes
*(delete as applicable)*

**Please send me:**            **Quantity**

New Daylight                   _____

New Daylight Large Print       _____

Guidelines                     _____

Day by Day with God            _____

*Please do not enclose payment. We have a fixed subscription year for Church Subscriptions,
which is from May to April each year. If you start a Church Subscription in the middle of a
subscription year, we will invoice you for the number of issues remaining in that year.*

# PBC ORDER FORM

**Please send me the following book(s):** | | Qty | Price | Total

| | | | |
|---|---|---|---|
| 030 8 PBC: 1 & 2 Samuel (H. Mowvley) | _____ | £7.99 | _____ |
| 118 5 PBC: 1 & 2 Kings (S. Dawes) | _____ | £7.99 | _____ |
| 070 7 PBC: Chronicles—Nehemiah (M. Tunnicliffe) | _____ | £7.99 | _____ |
| 031 6 PBC: Psalms 1—72 (D. Coggan) | _____ | £7.99 | _____ |
| 065 0 PBC: Psalms 73—150 (D. Coggan) | _____ | £7.99 | _____ |
| 071 5 PBC: Proverbs (E. Mellor) | _____ | £7.99 | _____ |
| 087 1 PBC: Jeremiah (R. Mason) | _____ | £7.99 | _____ |
| 028 6 PBC: Nahum—Malachi (G. Emmerson) | _____ | £7.99 | _____ |
| 191 6 PBC: Matthew (J. Proctor) | _____ | £7.99 | _____ |
| 046 4 PBC: Mark (D. France) | _____ | £7.99 | _____ |
| 027 8 PBC: Luke (H. Wansbrough) | _____ | £7.99 | _____ |
| 029 4 PBC: John (R.A. Burridge) | _____ | £7.99 | _____ |
| 082 0 PBC: Romans (J. Dunn) | _____ | £7.99 | _____ |
| 122 3 PBC: 1 Corinthians (J. Murphy-O'Connor) | _____ | £7.99 | _____ |
| 073 1 PBC: 2 Corinthians (A. Besançon Spencer) | _____ | £7.99 | _____ |
| 012 X PBC: Galatians and 1 & 2 Thessalonians (J. Fenton) | _____ | £7.99 | _____ |
| 047 2 PBC: Ephesians—Colossians & Philemon (M. Maxwell) | _____ | £7.99 | _____ |
| 119 3 PBC: Timothy, Titus and Hebrews (D. France) | _____ | £7.99 | _____ |
| 092 8 PBC: James—Jude (F. Moloney) | _____ | £7.99 | _____ |

## POSTAGE AND PACKING CHARGES

| order value | UK | Europe | Surface | Air Mail |
|---|---|---|---|---|
| £7.00 & under | £1.25 | £3.00 | £3.50 | £5.50 |
| £7.01–£30.00 | £2.25 | £5.50 | £6.50 | £10.00 |
| Over £30.00 | free | prices on request | | |

Total cost of books £ _____
Postage and packing £ _____
TOTAL £ _____

Please complete the payment details below and send your coupon, with appropriate payment to: BRF, First Floor, Elsfield Hall, 15–17 Elsfield Way, Oxford OX2 8FG.

Your name _____

Your address _____

_____

_____ Postcode _____

Total enclosed £ _____ (cheques should be made payable to 'BRF')

Payment by ☐ cheque   ☐ postal order   ☐ Visa   ☐ Mastercard   ☐ Switch

Card number: ☐☐☐☐☐☐☐☐☐☐☐☐☐☐☐☐☐☐☐☐

Expiry date of card: ☐☐☐☐      Issue number (Switch): ☐☐☐

Signature _____ Date   /   /
*(essential if paying by credit/Switch card)*

☐ Please do not mail me with other information about BRF

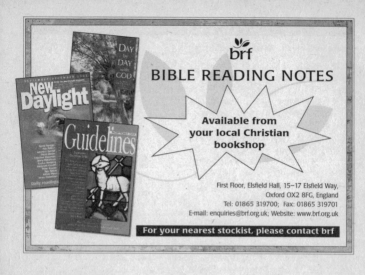

## BIBLE READING NOTES

**Available from your local Christian bookshop**

First Floor, Elsfield Hall, 15–17 Elsfield Way,
Oxford OX2 8FG, England
Tel: 01865 319700; Fax: 01865 319701
E-mail: enquiries@brf.org.uk; Website: www.brf.org.uk

**For your nearest stockist, please contact brf**

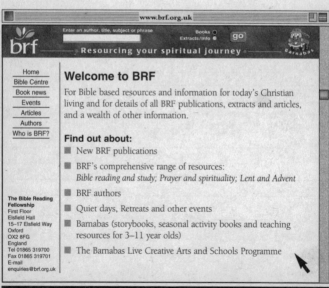